BORROWED BONES

NEW POEMS FROM THE
POET LAUREATE OF LOS ANGELES

—•—

LUIS J. RODRÍGUEZ

Foreword by Martín Espada

T0057588

CURBSTONE BOOKS
NORTHWESTERN UNIVERSITY PRESS
EVANSTON, ILLINOIS

Northwestern University Press
www.nupress.northwestern.edu

Copyright © 2016 by Luis J. Rodríguez. Foreword copyright © 2016
by Martín Espada. Published 2016 by Curbstone Books/Northwestern
University Press. All rights reserved.

Printed in the United States of America

10   9   8   7   6   5   4   3   2   1

Library of Congress Cataloging-in-Publication Data
Names: Rodriguez, Luis J., 1954– author.
Title: Borrowed bones : new poems from the poet laureate of Los Angeles /
    Luis J. Rodríguez ; foreword by Martín Espada.
Description: Evanston, Illinois : Curbstone Books/Northwestern
    University Press, 2016.
Identifiers: LCCN 2015045363 | ISBN 9780810133648 (pbk. : alk.
    paper)
Subjects: LCSH: Mexican Americans—Poetry.
Classification: LCC PS3568.O34879 B67 2016 | DDC 811.54—dc23
LC record available at http://lccn.loc.gov/2015045363

Dedicated to the
staff, board, volunteers, and community
of Tía Chucha's Cultural Center & Bookstore

"Where Art and Minds Meet—for a Change"

I breathed the air of so many places
without keeping a sample of any.
In the end, everyone is aware of this:
nobody keeps any of what he has,
and life is only a borrowing of bones.

—PABLO NERUDA

CONTENTS

Martín Espada

Long before he was named Poet Laureate of Los Angeles, Luis J. Rodríguez was doing what a laureate should do: serve the community.

Rodríguez empowers the community to speak for itself as the guiding spirit behind the dynamo called Tía Chucha's Centro Cultural and Bookstore in the Sylmar neighborhood of Los Angeles. Named for a favorite aunt, Tía Chucha's features everything from an annual "Celebrating Words" festival to open mikes (in English and Spanish), from workshops in writing, music, and puppetry to classes on indigenous languages and cosmology. This is the only trade bookstore serving half a million people in the Northeast San Fernando Valley. Their publishing wing, Tía Chucha Press, is one of the leading small press publishers of poetry in the country. Not by coincidence, Rodríguez has dedicated this collection of poems to Tía Chucha's "staff, board, volunteers, and community."

Rodríguez speaks on behalf of the community as a writer, with clarity, intensity, and integrity. This has been true since Tía Chucha published his *Poems across the Pavement* in 1989. Not long afterward, Sandy Taylor, the coeditor and copublisher of Curbstone Press, tossed a manuscript in my lap at his house on Jackson Street in Willimantic, Connecticut. I brushed Sandy's omnipresent cigarette ashes off the first page, and then the title caught my eye: *The Concrete River*. This was my introduction to the poems of Luis Rodríguez. "Tell me what you think," said Sandy. I read the manuscript in one sitting, struck by the soulful, brave revelations in the poems, by turns fierce and vulnerable, and gave it my vociferous approval. No doubt Sandy, keen judge of talent that he was, had already decided to publish the book. Curbstone published *The Concrete River* in 1991; it is appropriate, then, that Northwestern University Press has released *Borrowed Bones* as a Curbstone chapbook almost twenty-five years later.

One poem immediately leaps out at me from the pages of this collection: "Heavy Blue Veins: Watts, 1959." The image of the poet's mother, who "carefully cuts the engorged veins" on her ankles with a razor, bleeding them into a pail, was stunning when I first encountered the prose version of that description in *Always Running: La Vida Loca: Gang Days in*

L.A., the memoir Rodríguez published with Curbstone in 1993. (Sales of this bestselling book, and the rights, helped to subsidize other Curbstone books, mine included, for years afterward.) The poem articulates the unspoken pain and sacrifice of the poet's mother, translating his nightmares of blood into words that pay homage to her life of labor, reminding us that the work and the bleeding still go on today, in Los Angeles and beyond. The bloodletting and release of pent-up pain in the poem foreshadow the "riot" in Watts six years later, the first major urban uprising of the 1960s.

There is a deep sense of gratitude in these poems. Rodríguez is a poet who can claim, without hyperbole, that poetry saved his life, as, indeed, his poetry has saved others in their struggles with the streets, gangs, drugs, or incarceration. "Fevered Shapes" recalls the first reading he ever attended, in 1973, featuring José Montoya, David Henderson, and Pedro Pietri. (Pietri's *Puerto Rican Obituary* has influenced countless Puerto Rican writers, myself included.) After "half a dozen gun assaults, / cops knocking me around, / ODs, blades to my neck in jail cells," there is no greater shock for Rodríguez than the impact of the poets who transfix and transform him:

> They came for me and I've perspired poems
> ever since. They came for me—and all my addictions,
> my sorry-ass lies, my falling masks,
> my pissed-off wives, neglected children,
> angry friends, and back-to-back failures
> could never, ever, take them away.

There are echoes here of Pablo Neruda, recalling the way he discovered poetry, or, better put, the way poetry discovered him: "there I was without a face / and it touched me."

Luis Rodríguez is a poet of many tongues, befitting a city of many tongues. He speaks English, Spanish, "Hip Hop, the Blues," and "cool jazz." He speaks in "mad solos." He speaks in "People's Sonnets." He speaks in the language of protest. He speaks in the language of praise:

> Praise to shoes on a homeless winter night
> Praise to mothers who nurture without men
> Praise to the bottom in a drug-mad flight
> Praise to the poet who shatters with a pen

This poet embraces the city because he is the embodiment of the city. Witness his "Love Poem to Los Angeles." He knows well its sometimes "murderous heart," and refuses to romanticize. He sees clearly "the city of hungers, city of angers:"

> bone city, dried blood on walls,
> wildfires, taunting dove wails,
> car fumes and oil derricks,
> water thievery

He remembers wandering the landscape during the days of his "heroin-induced nods," sleeping in "abandoned cars" or "all-night movie showings / in downtown art deco theaters." He remembers the martyrs like Rubén Salazar, the Chicano journalist killed by a Los Angeles County Sheriff's deputy during the Chicano Moratorium march against the war in Vietnam.

Yet, this is a love poem. Rodríguez invokes the music and the musicians, famous and obscure: Richie Valens, Los Lobos, N.W.A., Charles Wright and the Watts 103rd Street Rhythm Band. He invokes the writers, celebrated and unsung: Charles Bukowski, Chester Himes, Wanda Coleman, John Fante, Marisela Norte. He invokes the relentless creative energy all around him: murals, lowriding, skateboarding. He invokes labor: the graveyard shifts. He invokes the natural world: the beaches, the palm trees, the wild parrots.

The poet is the city; the city is the poet. Thus, he writes in the spirit of another poet ancestor, Carl Sandburg, who wrote his *Chicago Poems* a century ago. Rodríguez lived in Chicago for fifteen years, won the Carl Sandburg Book Award, and included a poem about Chicago in this collection, "A Hungry Song in the Shadows." (What Sandburg called the "City of the Big Shoulders" Rodríguez calls "a city that steam built.")

Fifteen years ago, he came home. Now, as Poet Laureate of Los Angeles, Luis J. Rodríguez speaks eloquently of our "borrowed bones," mortality and the transcendence of mortality, for the poet, for the city, for all of us.

ACKNOWLEDGMENTS

Some of the poems in this chapbook previously appeared in the following publications, sometimes in other versions or under different titles:

Big Bridge Online Magazine (www.bigbridge.com): "Love Poems for Trini," Poetry by the Sea Series, Valentine's Day 2014, Malibu, Calif.

Blackmailpress (online): "Fevered Shapes," "Perhaps," "Machu Picchu—Or What I Should Have Become When the Ancient Stone Walls and the Clouded Heights Named My Blood," "Words"

The Brooklyn Rail: Critical Perspectives on Arts, Politics, and Culture: "People's State of the Union Sonnet"

Catamaran Literary Reader: "This Love" (from "Love Poems for Trini)

Edgar Allan Poet Journal #3: "The Dance Called La Trini" (from "Love Poems for Trini"), "Fevered Shapes," "Heavy Blue Veins: Watts, 1959," "Moonlight to Water"

Hinchas De Poesia (online literary magazine): "This Dance Known as La Trini" (from "Love Poems for Trini")

Homeboy Review: "Fevered Shapes," "Machu Picchu—Or What I Should Have Become When the Mountains Named My Blood," "Making Medicine," "Moonlight to Water," "Perhaps"

Huizache: The Magazine of Latino Literature: "Fevered Shapes," "Moonlight to Water"

Mas Tequila Review (Poetry for the rest of us): "Fevered Shapes"

Milestones: The Voices of East Los and Beyond: "Fevered Shapes," "Perhaps"

The People's Tribune: "Perhaps"

Platte River Review: "Moonlight to Water"

The Progressive Magazine: "The Healing Power of Poetry" (includes excerpt of poem "Fevered Shapes")

Statement Magazine: "Dance or Die"

Virginia Quarterly Review: "Fevered Shapes," "Heavy Blue Veins: Watts, 1959"

West Hollywood National Poetry Month Banner: From "Making Medicine": "The medicine is already inside us"

"A Hungry Song in the Shadows" was written for and displayed at the Jane Addams Hull House Museum in Chicago for the Alternative Labeling Project, cosponsored by the Poetry Foundation.

"Making Medicine" was first published as a handmade limited edition and numbered art book (Pajaro, Calif.: C&C Press, 2007). A few poems appeared as prose in the memoirs *Always Running, La Vida Loca, Gang Days in L.A.* (Curbstone Press, 1993; Touchstone Books/Simon & Schuster, 1994) and *It Calls You Back: An Odyssey through Love, Addiction, Revolution, and Healing* (Touchstone Books/Simon & Schuster, 2011) as well as in my fiction, *The Republic of East Los Angeles: Stories* (Rayo Books/HarperCollins, 2002) and *Music of the Mill: A Novel* (Rayo Books/HarperCollins, 2005).

"People's Sonnets" was published in *Overthrowing Capitalism: Beyond Endless War, Racist Police, Sexist Elites* (San Francisco: Kallatumba Press, 2015).

"Perhaps" was published in *The Poetry Circus* (Littlerock, Calif.: Yak Press, 2015).

WORDS

The thing is I wanted to be a writer
even before I knew what writing was about.
I wanted to carve out the words
that swim in the bloodstream,
to press a stunted pencil onto paper
so lines break free like birds in flight—
to fashion words with hair,
lengths and lengths of it,
washed with dawn's rusting drizzle.

I yearned for mortar-lined words,
speaking in their own boasting tongues,
not the diminished, frightened stammering of my childhood,
but to shape scorching syllables with midnight dust.
Words that stood up in bed,
danced *merenques* and *cumbias*,
that incinerated the belly like a shimmering *habanera*.
Words with a spoonful of tears, buckshot, traces of garlic,
cilantro, aerosol spray, and ocean froth.
Words that guffawed, tarnished smooth faces,
and wrung song out of silence.

Words as languid as a woman's stride,
as severe as a convict's gaze,
herniated like a bad plan,
soaked as in a summer downpour.

I aspired to walk inside these words,
to manipulate their internal organs,
surrounded by veins, gray matter, and caesuras;
to slam words down like the bones of a street domino game—
and to crack them in two like lovers' hearts.

HEAVY BLUE VEINS: WATTS, 1959

Heavy blue veins streak across my mother's legs,
Some of them bunched up into dark lumps at her ankles.
Mama periodically bleeds them to relieve the pain.
She carefully cuts the engorged veins with a razor
And drains them into a porcelainlike metal pail
Called a *tina*.
I'm small and all I remember are dreams of blood,
Me drowning in a red sea, blood on sheets, on the walls,
Splashing against the white pail in streams
Out of my mother's ankle.
But they aren't dreams.
It is Mama bleeding—into day, into night.
Bleeding a birth of memory: my mother, my blood,
By the side of the bed, me on the covers,
And her slicing into a black vein
And filling the pail into some dark, forbidding
Red nightmare, which never stops coming,
Nevers stops pouring,
This memory of Mama and blood and Watts.

MAKING MEDICINE

A bee makes love to a flower.
There's more dark matter
in the universe than light.
What may kill you may also cure you.
Look around—there's medicine everywhere.

Change is the medicine of the stagnant
and what seems changeless.

So ask the questions:

If society cooperates, can we nurture the full
and healthy development of everyone?

If the world loses its soul,
shouldn't we imagine another world
from the depths of all our souls?

Is there a truth that also stings?

The journey emerges from the folds of an ocean wave
lapping at the shores of entangled blood.
It's the music rejoicing release at the throat,
a moon-faced declaration suggesting
the night's winged descent toward a wound.

Truths that heal are expressed in poems
that breathe and hold
the air in the eye sockets
of a deadened smile;

truths with muddy roads, vacant stares,
and broken glass windows;

truths with a girl's tinny laugh
in the cuddle of her mother's fears
in the sleep of her pregnant winters;

truth that is stubborn peace, hobbling wet along
a forest of bare and calamitous trees,
immersed in the salt of a thousand dry kisses.

Like how music squeezes out the lunacy
in our hearts, how the happiest moments
are usually the least complicated,
and how love is felt in the creases
of our fingers,
but no hand can carry.

So heal with these bullets,
tunes that twist a word, a phrase,
a notion to poetic slaughter;
heal with a hunger that is also
the ceaseless babble for what's just.

We can't swat away the madness in these words,
to sear black the books and dictionaries
of these sorrows and secrets;
we can't harmonize with the scorned instruments
whose language falls into a mouth
bursting red with the melodies of dissent
like whispers in a bottle.

Roots and songs fall in the chasms
between the disconnections,
making medicine out of our disaffections
and alienations,
our pathologies and poverties.

History is a series of explosions;
in between we dream.

The truth is—the medicine
is already inside us.

Meander then around the hollowed possessions,
through these featherless borders,
in a cauldron of holy oil and the devil's piss,
and always,
always,
ask the questions.

MOONLIGHT TO WATER

(For my youngest sons, Ruben and Luis)

Ruben recalled the day I brought Mama
and his baby brother home when he was six.
In the back seat of the car, he said,
was an Asian looking child,
hair sticking straight up on his head.

Chito—short for *Luisito*—looked this way
because he's part Rarámuri and Huichol,
but mostly all universe.
Ruben must have wondered about the galaxy of stars,
bird songs, and stories that had been dreamt
to fashion such a boy.

When Chito arrived I'm sure Ruben knew
his world would never be the same.

Until then, Ruben had been our only child.
To mom and dad, he was the screech
of car brakes,
a sigh to a bad joke,
the glove to our ball,
and now this—a bewildered boy gazing
at a sweet-faced earth child
wrapped in a light-blue blanket.

I asked Ruben what he thought about his brother.
Eyes gleaming with a six-year-old's clarity,
he answered: "Oh, I already knew him—
I saw Chito when I was in Mama's stomach."

I gave Ruben a look I often offered
in reply to his amazing observations.
Somehow, though, the statement rang true.
His younger brother was in the wings,
preparing to part, the next one,
patiently abiding his turn.

As they grew older, Chito followed his brother's
every move, entering wide-eyed
into Ruben's dense sphere,
sharing the same music, games, imaginings.

Ruben never hurt or exploited him,
as older brothers often do.

The boys connected from the start,
like hummingbird to flower,
like breath to poems,
like moonlight to water,
brothers since the womb.

FEVERED SHAPES

*(For Jose Montoya, David Henderson, and Pedro Pietri and the
first poetry reading I ever attended, autumn 1973)*

I wallowed in a needle-spawned world,
addicted to dope and the crazy life,
and yet there I was—in Berkeley
for my first poetry reading.

I was eighteen—with a bullet, as they say.
Earlier I had flown on a plane for the first time.
Sure I've survived half a dozen gun assaults,
cops knocking me around,
ODs, blades to my neck in jail cells,
homelessness in dank streets,
and beat downs in barrio brawls—but flying?
That scared me to death.

I sat there in a crowded cafe,
not knowing what to expect.
Poetry? I'd never heard this before.
Oh, I had written lines:
vignettes, images, fears, thoughts.
I didn't know they were poems.

I had no idea what a poem was.

First up on the mic was Jose Montoya,
with Chicano prayers of old *pachucos*,
and strained loves and guitar solos,
and Indian hands in corn flour.

Then David Henderson took the stage,
gleaning urban black streets, racist stares,
Black Panther fury and Southern cooking.

Finally, Pedro Pietri came up—Nuyorican
word *meister*, flashing El Barrio's experiences
with poems located in phone booths and real-life wisdoms
that made us laugh and shake our heads.

I had never heard words spoken this way,
more music than talk,
more fevered shapes than sentences,
more Che and Malcolm than Shakespeare.

These poems came for me,
lassoed my throat,
demanded my life's savings,
taking me for a sunset ride.

These poems were graffiti scrawls
along the alleys and trash-strewn tunnels of my body,
the metaphoric methadone for the heroin hurling
through my bloodstream, the lifeline I already had inside
and didn't know.

These poems were pool sticks, darkened gangways,
a swirl of sunrise after the graveyard shift,
a blood-black yelling behind torn curtains,
a child shrieking and nobody coming to help.

They were a woman's scent after a night
of lovemaking, a sweet touch of hand to face,
cascades of hair on a pillow,
a moan during an elongated kiss.

These poems were shadowed intents,
startled doubts, sorrows without grief,
the moon without sky,
unknown melodies . . .
the falling inside that happens
when you push razor onto wrist.

They came for me as I sank into my suicide,
while fidgeting in a chair,
inching under the skin,
as I wondered why I even came.

Jose, David, and Pedro—
I was never the same after this.
They came for me and I've never let go.
They came for me and I've perspired poems
ever since. They came for me—and all my addictions,
my sorry-ass lies, my falling masks,
my pissed-off wives, neglected children,
angry friends, and back-to-back failures
could never, ever, take them away.

DANCE OR DIE

(For the Rarámuri people of Chihuahua, Mexico)

1

When the world stops its collective rituals,
ignoring the red-burn indictments
of its wounded and betrayed;
when it pushes out the verses of life
and holds back the celebrations that mark
our staggered steps to awareness;
when it impedes the subtle earth incantations,
plowing over the wild open terrains of the heart,
blocking the creative soul-depth birthing;
when it forces our home, our earth, to become
mucus-clay to whatever deadly energies can burn through,
forcing glaciers to tumble, forests to yield,
oceans to churn; when diamonds, gold, oil, cars—
and homes too big for ten families,
let alone one—can boom,
but respect, dignity, community
are hard to come by . . .
then somebody
has to dance
to keep everything
from dying.

2

In the Copper Canyon of old Chihuahua,
some eighty thousand Rarámuri people live,
hidden among the volcanic rocks and pine trees—
one of the last tribes of cave-dwellers in the world.

I visited the Rarámuri one Mexican summer
with a Navajo friend,
who wanted to witness this cohesive and ancient tribe,
which existed the way his people had more than a hundred years before.

We slept in caves,
washed and cooked without electricity,
battled growling mangy dogs.
We also met remarkably shy, but calm and connected
people of the corn.

Still most of the Rarámuri were desperate:
hungry, neglected, hunted.
The caves were their last refuge.

3

Among the more traditional Rarámuri
there's a concept—to dance or die.
They feel they must carry out rituals
for the rest of us since our so-called civilization
has forgotten what it knew.
We have lost our essence to industry,
to capital, to stolen labor.
We've forgotten how to respect and honor relationships,
the nature inside and around us,
and how these relationships held in balance
allow for abundance and renewal.

We've turned away from these laws,
forcing the earth to go beyond its healing capacities,
placing superficial needs over the deeply human,
the man-made, or man-mad, over nature's,
which always makes sense,
always rhymes,
always reasons.

We can save the world yet,
but somebody has to maintain the songs,
the invocations,
the delights.

Somebody has to keep dancing.

PERHAPS

Perhaps when the stories are lost and pleasure is a dry river
and what makes the flesh sing is a long-gone supplication,
we may find our true names.

Perhaps when the earth's rotation stops, when the moon has wilted,
and the sun's rays scorch down this squandered ground,
we may uncover our inner eye.

Perhaps when the poisons that once were our sustenance
and the radiation that once gave us light, now foster
our insatiable hungers and an abiding darkness,
we may know what really feeds and guides us.

Perhaps after we've created so many borders, so many walls,
and conjured up even more laws to make even more lawless,
we may realize it's ourselves who've been made illegal,
it's our spirits we've alienized.

Perhaps when parents lose their final grasps on their children,
they will finally grasp that their sole purpose is to bring loved, healthy,
and understood children into this world—to remake
the universe, better and more holy each time.

Perhaps when the wars in the names of countless gods,
which look and act like those who evoke them, finally end,
we may realize that God is the unnamable, unobtrusive wind
that caresses our cheeks, the rain that falls on us all,
the air that enters our lungs, and the nerves in our brains
so we can name whatever God we want.

Perhaps when all the textbooks and written histories
and science papers cease, we'll understand that nature,

and our own natures, are the source of all knowledge,
language, and histories, and we'll always be able to rewrite them,
reimagine them, and reweave them into the world.

Perhaps when love has become the embers of what we hate,
the residue of what we've destroyed, we'll know that love
is the stream that flows through each and every one of us,
the water we thirst for in the deserts of our days,
the ocean from which all our tears,
full of salt and unmet desires,
surge and flow.

MACHU PICCHU—OR WHAT I SHOULD HAVE BECOME WHEN THE ANCIENT STONE WALLS AND THE CLOUDED HEIGHTS NAMED MY BLOOD

memories of childhood rise up like a twisted vine,
mocking the granite sinews of this adult body and the solid layers of lies
that have become my face, demanding a lightness of foot and of fears
as antidotes to the round-bellied night crawler
I've succumbed to—this clown in tattooed skin,
a priest without prayers, the wrinkled figure in soggy coat
   on a scorched plain

fire awakens me although I'm cold inside,
surrounded by carcasses of embattled loves
and blistered stories, always ending with betrayals and dismissals,
with the turning away of the most emblazoned eye;
they are the settled unholy ingredients in the bottled angst I've traded
on street corners, poetry bars, living room arguments,
and between the multi-tracked songs that singe
   the cluttered paths of my lunacies

I can't hide, I can't run, the ruins speak to me in whispered cadences,
with scrolled breath, blurting out curative threats,
words that bob and weave in a rushing mud river,
ripping the flesh of cruel invectives, addressing me like a worried mother,
a tired frog outside my window, while laying me down on a ground
crawling with spiders and my best intentions

I learned to live on chicken and vegetable soups,
long walks, coca leaves inside my cheeks, *chicha morada*,
the way the natives did for thousands of years, with few calories,

yet still energized, awake, strong, and even the wooded hills
and high altitudes are less formidable, less monstrous, more like brothers,
like leaves, like a welcoming breeze

Machu Picchu, you were always in my crowded
dreams, in the faded colors of my worn clothes,
on the folds near my eyes, always a tree branch
to cling to, a father when my own father ate the hearts of his children,
as a brother in the heroin-nights of my downtowns,
even when I had never seen you

I'm here and I sense this open citadel helped shape my hands,
my mouth, the many constants of my inconsistencies,
and whatever death melody I played but never died to

a place, an embrace, a cauldron of history I never knew I had,
Machu Picchu survived the thousands for my steps to seal this pact,
to communicate what winds and tortured rain cannot do,
as a meditation in stone, moss, and cloud,
with six-inch *colibri* and saddened flower to accompany me,
climbing the heights of this carved womb on a grinning mountain
to the depths of my own negations and hypocrisies,
to whatever song suggests my slow and languid
tearing out of my skin

A HUNGRY SONG IN THE SHADOWS

(For Chicago)

When I think about Chicago's first settlers, migrants, jobseekers,
    who sought haven or the hope of one,

I think about a place fierce with wails, noises in all decibels,
    tongues from all reaches, and how this is not just a city,

but a dream state of brick and chain-link fences, where poetry clatters
    along with the El train on iron rails, where temples hold every

belief and street corners every color, a city that nourishes all palates,
    holds all thoughts, and still contains the seed of this vital idea:

in accord with nature, all is possible. This is a city that steam built.
    That muscle and sweat solidified into a church

of organized labor. Where a swampy onion field in a few generations
    could become home to the brightest and most jagged skyline,

where fossil fuels are holy water and smokestacks and silos remain
    as soot-stained monuments to industry—from horse-drawn plows,

to the foulest stockyards, the roar of combustion engines, the clang
    of metal-tipped tools, and smoke-curling big rigs streaming along

cluttered expressways and upturned streets. I came to this city on my knees,
    laden with heartaches, bitter in the shadows, seeking a thousand voices

that speak in one voice, where steel no longer reigns, but where open mics
    and poetry slams keep the steel in our verses, lamenting a life of work,

in a time of no work, and where the inventive and inspiring
could finally burst through the cement viaducts and snowy terrains.

Now we are artists or we die. From the fractured neighborhoods where
bootblacks and news hawking boys once held sway, to this daunting

gentrified metropolis of ghosts, toxic waste, and countless poor ripped
from their housing projects, three-flat graystones, or trash-lined

bungalows, yet nothing can truly uproot the uprooted. The energy for what
Chicago can become is buried inside people, in callings, passions,

and technologies, but only if this manufactured garden aligns
with real nature, no longer limited, finite, fixed on scarcity, but abundant,

cooperative, regenerative, like a song across the lakeshore, blooming
with lights, music, dance, banners, and words into a cornucopia

of potentials, possibilities, even the impossible. It's an imagination
for the intrinsic beauty and bounty in all things.

Chicago. Clean. Just. Free. It's the city we've wept and bled to see.

WHEN A POET APPEARS . . .

When a poet appears the earth springs into song
Flowered with new hope,
A bright beginning even from a terribly seeded past
Where dust and stones are a bare sowing ground.

Poets know there's a design to their lives.
Braided with threads of the future
They don't just make and remake language,
They are called to it—just as a solid and direct line
Can become fleeting or slanted.

Aspiring to be a poet, you become a poet,
Turning what's possible into what's next.

Not just creating a nest for oneself
Made of familiar sounds that keep one comfortable,

Not just basking in the spotlight or the imagined power,

But by cultivating words with courage, discipline,
And ferocity—
Poets carry this sacrifice with grace.

Always remember the unrecoverable moments,
With loved ones—with family—
While also giving to the whole
Even at the expense of one's time,
One's considerations.

All proper sacrifices are rooted in the sacred.

Blessed and cursed,
Loved and hated,
Seen well or lied about,
No poet can escape the human energies
That both destroy and lift up.

Yet true poets are matched for this challenge.
There is a poet-seed planted
Before birth and carefully nurtured
By angels
By elements
By the alignments of universal sway.

You feel this in the bones—somewhere the message is:
"I was meant to be here."

The fact is poetry is in everyone:
It emerges from the human sea.

Yet, as deeper truths go,
Poets see farther and feel deeper:
Just like the rest of us, only maybe more,
Turning time into learning, into passion, into revelation.

They bargain with God for how to be in the world:
Learning for learning,
Passion for passion—
Revelation for revelation.

LOVE POEMS FOR TRINI

When Trini and I found our time, we had closed in on almost ten years of meeting each other. We discovered correlations between us, but did not always recognize—what dew made up our mornings, what moon settled into our laughs, what water lapped at our shores. It seemed that superior hands were molding this enterprise, as if the other world were orchestrating our music, tender or harsh, full of dense rhythms, yet habitually in harmony. Maybe it was the spirits of our two sons from the future, scrutinizing our coming together, our breakups, our kisses, our angers, as if the boys were at the controls of some unearthly video game, exasperated at the hesitations, fears, and indiscretions, yet pulling at us, coaxing us, slamming us . . . *damn, Mom, Dad, be kind to each other. Be in love, for Christ's sake. This is serious—we can't exist without you.*

We now have thirty years as a couple with our sons born, parented, now grown up—healthy, strong, exceptional. Somehow we mastered the turns, despite the roadblocks, the wrong ways, those periods when we stood paralyzed, wasting songs, shattering into pieces, trying to make the jagged portions fit again. This is a bond made of bright and torn fabric, a whimsical joke, a slow dance, a stinging salsa, a good cup of coffee—also of nights without sleep, raging storms, the silences, the long walks, the secrets-unraveling talks.

Our love is a missive from the future, with frayed strands from the past, and an ever-incandescent glow in the womb of our present. Thanks Sons, thanks Sun, thanks birds, thanks moon, thanks all blooming. We've made our way.

2

This love is not what you think love is . . .

This love is not to be messed with, misunderstood, or underestimated

This love is not a stairway or a feather or a lingering doubt

This love is oatmeal breakfasts, walks with our dog, holding hands in the mall, kissing every time as if it were our first, opening the doors to our visiting sons

This love is her laughing at my unfunny jests—and me floored by her clever ones

This love is admiring the way our brains work, our hearts feel, our skin responds, how our tones ignite a pulsing breath from a longing depth

This love is respect squared, dignity shared, a steel railing over rustic steps, a dry alcove when it rains

It's an eternal locomotive of caring, what rustling a tranquil breeze unleashes, the way a sunbeam flickers on a rushing stream

This love is afternoon *raspadas*, whispers in the park, Ferris wheel rides, a stroll in a darkened museum

It's a madjoyscreamingbinge—intoxicated with auras of faces when we're not there, and how teardrops rip open the heart's flesh when we are

This love cannot be colorized, hung out to dry, or pushed off the road

It's not a bookmark, a clock without hands, or the white of your eyes

What you think this love is, it's probably not.

3

There's a dance that is like running,
a sprint inside a glance,
a dance that belongs to La Trini.
The body swivels through space and emotions,
through dread and sweet hugs,
through next-morning doubts and wild lips on skin.
This dance is surrender, a bitter douse of memory,
also honey shimmering across a night sky.

There is a dance called La Trini,
perfect steps in an imperfect world.
She dances and the world is clay in her hands.
She dances and the limbs become liberated and agile.
She dances and it's a flight through the mystery of hugs,
infused by the particular solace of being held
and a strange shame in not knowing how to let go.

There's a dance known only to La Trini,
a secret song in the folds of a battered self,
how in time it becomes nuanced,
with measured moments,
surprising even the dancer.

Some days the dance is a wayward waltz,
an unmannered minuet, yet still a sure glide
into the arms of a partner in rhyme,
a partner synchronized,
whose unsure footing and missteps
finally plummet into line with this love,
this woman, this dance named Trini.

AN OBSERVATION

My mother, with Rarámuri roots, born in Chihuahua, Mexico,
acquired Alzheimer's disease in her seventies—
a woman of stories forgetting her story.
She passed on before she failed to remember me.
In my saddened state, her death proved a blessing.
A naturalized U.S. citizen, who loved this country,
although she never learned English,
my mother died in a U.S. hospital
with the American Dream in her heart, if not in mind.
I have a son, one of four children, whom teachers declared to be "troubled,"
rambunctious (aren't they all?). This was in kindergarten.
These adults claimed he needed Ritalin for attention deficit disorder.
My son had ADD and my mother had AD.
Yet isn't this the state of our culture, unable to focus, forced to forget?
Death resolved my mother's affliction.
A Native American focus program dealt with my son's.
But America's afflictions are more intractable.
With all our belief systems, certainties, moral compasses,
we remain unsure, memoryless, disoriented.

LOVE POEM TO LOS ANGELES

(with a respectful nod to Jack Hirschman)

1

To say I love Los Angeles is to say
I love its shadows and nightlights,
its meandering streets,
the stretch of sunset-colored beaches.
It's to say I love the squawking wild parrots,
the palm trees that fail to topple in robust winds,
that within a half hour of L.A.'s center
you can cavort in snow, deserts, mountains, beaches.

This is a multi-layered city,
unceremoniously built on hills,
valleys, ravines.
Flying into Burbank airport in the day,
you observe gradations of trees and earth.
A "city" seems to be an afterthought,
skyscrapers popping up from the greenery,
guarded by the mighty San Gabriels.

2

Layers of history reach deep,
run red, scarring the soul of the city,
a land where Chinese were lynched,
Mexican resistance fighters hounded,
workers and immigrants exploited,
Japanese removed to concentration camps,
blacks forced from farmlands in the South,
then segregated, diminished.

Here also are blessed native lands,
where first peoples like the Tataviam and Tongva
bonded with nature's gifts;
people of peace, deep stature, loving hands.
Yet for all my love
I also abhor the "poison" time,
starting with Spanish settlers, the Missions,
where 80 percent of natives
who lived and worked in them died,
to the ruthless murder of Indians
during and after the Gold Rush,
the worst slaughter of tribes in the country.

From all manner of uprisings,
a city of acceptance began to emerge.
This is "riot city" after all—
more civil disturbances in Los Angeles
in the past hundred years
than any other city.

3

To truly love L.A. you have to see it
with different eyes,
askew perhaps,
beyond the fantasy-induced Hollywood spectacles.
"El Lay" is also known
for the most violent street gangs,
the largest Skid Row,
the greatest number of poor.

Yet I loved L.A.
even during heroin-induced nods
or running down rain-soaked alleys or getting shot at.
Even when I slept in abandoned cars,
alongside the "concrete" river,

and during all-night movie showings
in downtown art deco theaters.
The city beckoned as I tried to escape
the prison-like grip of its shallowness,
sun-soaked image, suburban quiet,
all disarming,
hiding the murderous heart
that can beat at its center.

L.A. is also lovers' embraces,
the most magnificent lies,
the largest commercial ports,
graveyard shifts,
poetry readings,
murals,
lowriding culture,
skateboarding,
a sound that hybridized
black, Mexican, as well as Asian
and white migrant cultures.

You wouldn't have musicians like
Ritchie Valens, The Doors, War,
Los Lobos, Charles Wright &
the Watts 103rd Street Rhythm Band,
Hiroshima, Motley Crue, N.W.A., or Quetzal
without Los Angeles.

Or John Fante, Chester Himes, Charles Bukowski,
Marisela Norte, and Wanda Coleman as its jester poets.

4

I love L.A., I can't forget its smells,
I love to make love in L.A.,
it's a great city, a city without a handle,

the world's most mixed metropolis,
of intolerance and divisions,
how I love it, how I hate it,
Zootsuit "riots,"
can't stay away,
city of hungers, city of angers,
Ruben Salazar, Rodney King,
I'd like to kick *its* face in,
bone city, dried blood on walls,
wildfires, taunting dove wails,
car fumes and oil derricks,
water thievery,
with every industry possible
and still a "one-industry town,"
lined by those majestic palm trees
and like its people
with solid roots, supple trunks,
resilient.

PEOPLE'S SONNETS

1

A shadow hangs where my country should glow.
Despite glories shaped as skyscrapers or sound.
More wars, more prisons, less safe, still low.
Massive cities teeter on shifting ground.
Glittering lights, music tracks hide the craven.
TV, movies, books so we can forget.
Countless worn out, debt-laden and slaving;
Their soul-derived destinies unmet.
Give me NASCAR, lowriders, Hip Hop, the Blues.
Give me Crooklyn, cowboys, cool jazz, cholos.
Give me libraries, gardens of the muse.
Give me songs over sidewalks, mad solos.
      Big America improperly sized.
      Give me your true value, realized.

2

Praise to shoes on a homeless winter night
Praise to mothers who nurture without men
Praise to the bottom in a drug-mad flight
Praise to the poet who shatters with a pen
Praise to vibrant children in a static world
Praise to dreamers in cash-only exchanges
Praise to the tattered flag of justice, unfurled
Praise to our nation's depth, breadth, and ranges
Praise to a restoring earth with global warming
Praise to large spirits even in cages
Praise to the new alignments now forming
Praise to anger with eyes, not blind rages
      There is much to praise, if we are to last
      The big within the small, the small in the vast

3

God is everywhere, for everyone,
on rosy petal and butterfly wing,
in colors on water split by the sun,
across the blue-gray of sky as birds sing.
Yet how many have pinned God to a wall:
stuffing it tight into a shotgun shell,
denim and flannel, shopping on the mall,
scowl-faced and wrathful, less heaven, more hell.
God's no longer free, loving, or female.
He's cradling a rifle on the border,
modifying crops, fracking oil from shale.
This God's for profits, a new world order.
      Where's Great Spirit for all, not judge or king,
      accepting, welcoming, all life's wellspring?

4

I'm for peace as war rages around us,
for paintbrushes, guitars instead of guns,
for murals, theaters, venues to discuss,
to share, teach, pushing out lyrical runs.
Today we sing amidst a mother's dark screams,
sounds often drowning out any sonatas,
time now for harmony, lasting brave dreams,
all mothers heard, *todas encantadas*.
Unceasing joy from deep and prevailing ties,
lacing together detached and sick lives.
No more pushed off laments or censored cries;
all should thrive, not gamble on who survives.
      Peace in a time of peace, bounty's call.
      Everybody recognized, striding tall.

5

Let us dare haunting verse of the oppressed,
poems with hoodies, finger-tapping, ambling.
I mean pissed off and ardently expressed,
poems delirious as midnight rambling.
Bebop, Hip Hop, a *decima* or slam,
metered lyrics, free shaped texts . . . no matter,
bring out the fire, the punch, a resounding jam.
Let it ring far, a magnificent chatter.
Naming the nameless, voicing the unheard,
questioning the questions, swimming, splashing.
No expert strokes but damn if not expert word;
every line bleeding, grieving, pleading, slashing.
> The power of poetry is its stance,
> page or stage, electrifying or trance.

6

The country is rent with discord, dissent:
police killings, new prisons, much to deplore.
Even with tax dollars mindlessly spent:
climate fails, poverty, injustice, and war.
Some take sides, split the common people,
arguing to the death their issue is key.
Connect the dots—temple, mosque, or steeple.
Same source means common aims to be free.
Healthy, blooming, embracing communities—
is this so hard to imagine for all?
We may disagree, still there are unities;
we may move slow, but on two legs, not crawl.
> None of these issues can be solved alone.
> Prepare to learn more, this much is known.

Los Angeles Mayor Eric Garcetti chose Luis J. Rodríguez as Poet Laureate of the city in 2014. Rodríguez is Scholar-in-Residence at California State University, Northridge, and the author of fifteen books of poetry, children's literature, fiction, and nonfiction. For more than thirty-five years, he has been speaking and reading at schools, libraries, conferences, prisons, juvenile lockups, homeless shelters, migrant camps, and Native American reservations in the United States, as well as at festivals, book fairs, colleges, and universities throughout North, Central, and South America; the Caribbean; Europe; and Japan.

Rodríguez won a 2015 Paterson Award for Sustained Literary Achievement for *Poems across the Pavement: 25th Anniversary Edition*. His awards also include a PEN Josephine Miles Literary Award, a Paterson Poetry Prize, a Carl Sandburg Literary Award, and fellowships from the Sundance Institute, the Lannan Foundation, the City of Los Angeles, the City of Chicago, the California Arts Council, and the Illinois Arts Council.

The 1993 memoir *Always Running, La Vida Loca, Gang Days in L.A.*, with close to half a million copies sold, became one of L.A.'s most checked out in libraries—and one of the most stolen. His memoir *It Calls You Back: An Odyssey through Love, Addiction, Revolutions, and Healing* was a finalist for the 2012 National Book Critics Circle Award.

In Chicago, where he lived from 1985 to 2000, Rodríguez was active in the poetry slam movement born there. He was cofounder of the Guild Complex Literary Center, an organizer for the Neutral Turf Poetry Festival, and a writer for the city's poetry magazine *Letter eX*. In 1993, Rodríguez took part in the first Slam Poetry tour of Europe. He also founded the crosscultural small press, Tía Chucha, now publishing for more than twenty-five years.

After moving back to Los Angeles, Rodríguez, his wife Trini, and other family and community members created Tía Chucha's Centro Cultural & Bookstore in the San Fernando Valley, offering workshops in the arts, writing, dance, theater, photography, indigenous cosmology and language, and encompassing arts and literacy festivals, an art gallery, weekly open mics, performance space, and a bookstore.